Forward Motion...
the Keys to Progress & Success!

By Dr. Alfred S. Titus, Jr.

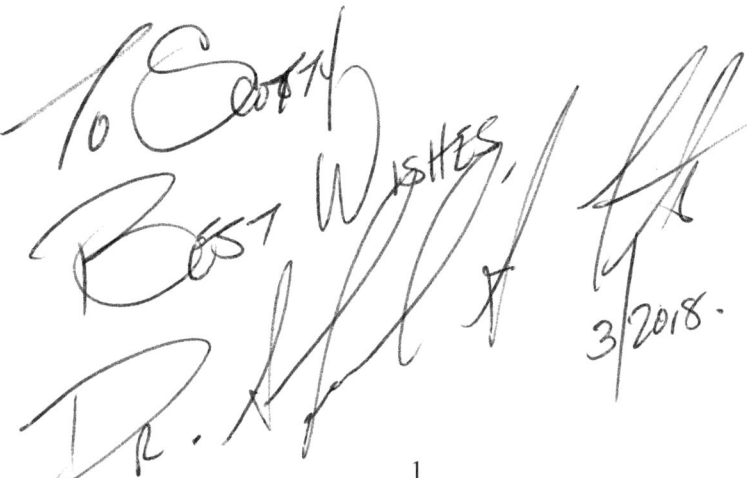

Forward Motion…

the Keys to Progress and Success

Copyright © 2017 by Dr. Alfred S. Titus, Jr.

All rights reserved. No part of this book may be used or reproduced by any means – graphic, electronic, or mechanical, including photocopying, recording, taping, or any information storage retrieval system – without the written permission of the author except in the case of brief quotations embodied in critical articles and reviews.

ISBN: 9781973553038 (paperback)

Dedication

THIS BOOK IS DEDICATED
TO MY THREE CHILDREN:
TIFFANY, BRIANNA, AND MICHAEL…
MY GREATEST JOYS!

MY CHILDREN
HAVE ALWAYS BEEN
THE INSPIRATION FOR ALL THAT I DO
AND ALL THAT I ACCOMPLISH.

THEIR MERE EXISTENCE
PROVIDES ME WITH THE STRENGTH,
DETERMINATION, AND MOTIVATION
TO CONQUER
ALL OBSTACLES AND BARRIERS.

TO SET AN EXAMPLE
FOR THEM TO FOLLOW,
TO KNOW THAT THERE ARE
NO LIMITS IN LIFE –
THAT IS MY GOAL!

REACH FOR THE STARS!!!

Forward Motion...

the Keys to Progress and Success!
By Dr. Alfred S. Titus, Jr.

Chapters

FOREWORD.. 7

INTRODUCTION..13

1. DREAMS DEFERRED: FEARS & AMBITION.........16
2. SPOUSES, PARTNERS, & FAMILY....................30
3. FRIENDS & THE COMPANY WE KEEP...............35
4. DRUGS, ALCOHOL, & OTHER VICES...............45
5. EDUCATION..50
6. RUNNING SOLO......................................58
7. DON'T SWEAT THE SMALL THINKING –
   LEVELING SIGNIFICANCE...........................63
8. MOTIVATION – FIND YOURS.......................68
9. THE DOWNSIDE OF AMBITION.....................81
10. NEVER GIVE UP! NEVER!..........................86
11. FINAL THOUGHTS... IN CONCLUSION.............90
12. ABOUT THE AUTHOR................................94

Foreword

The inspiration for this book comes from the numerous experiences and situations I've been lucky enough to survive throughout my life. My experiences, some of which are revealed in this book, will detail the lessons learned and will illustrate how your future can be affected by the people, places, and things that are part of your surroundings. The lessons learned are from my experiences in the streets, in college, in public service, and throughout my life.

With each experience comes an extraordinary opportunity to learn and grow. That is if you are the type of person to recognize and learn from experiences. Not everyone is that person. I have been blessed with the ability to be a deep thinker, a planner, and a very observant person. I believe this comes from the numerous lectures and talks my mother bestowed upon me while growing up. The talks with my mother made a lasting impression on me. The lectures provided me with the insight to put thought into every endeavor, to look ahead, and to thoroughly think things through before acting.

Although each experience has been essential, the ones that have been the most meaningful and confirming for me were the experiences I gained through my 23 years in public service. By confirming, I mean the experiences and lessons I learned upheld what I was taught, suspected, or already knew. Although not every lesson pertains to the information in this book, the ones that relate to success are included here. However, from time to time, some of the lessons will relate to personal life issues.

The most valuable experiences and lessons I learned were during my former career as a police officer, detective, and hostage negotiator with the New York City Police Department. Most people who have grown up in a specific area, may expand out of the area for work or school, but never really get to see every aspect of society. Society, or the world to most, is what they see in their small circle, on the news, on television, in the movies, or read in books. Working in public service and dealing with people from all walks of life, sometimes in the most adverse situations, has allowed me to see one common thread: the desire to succeed, to be successful.

Some may disagree with the previous statement. Some may say that many people are content with where they are, content with what they have, and have no desire to work hard to get more. I disagree. I feel that even those who appear not to be willing to work hard to get that bigger life, that extra money, etc., still want all of those things. They may be more afraid than most, feel that their lack of education or financial situation may not put them in the running, think that their position in life makes it impossible for them to succeed, or they may not be aware of the steps and the resources available to them. In fact, the issue can boil down to a feeling of inadequacy, a feeling that they will embarrass themselves if they try and fail, and people will laugh at them for even trying – that people will say, what made you think you could do that, have that, or become that?

We all want success. In some way, shape, or form, every one of us wants to be successful at something. Some dream of success and never try to achieve it. Some dream of success and try shortcuts to achieve it. Others try a few times, fail, and give up. Then there are those who want, try, fail, try again, fail, and try again – over and over again, hoping that one day one of their attempts will propel them to success. This book is written for everyone who wants success, needs the push, the refocus, and the reassurance. Those who need to know whether what they are doing is right or wrong.

This book is for all the young men and women who feel lost in this big world, who have no idea which direction they should take, who are confused about their options and are standing still in uncertainty. This book is for all the adults who are afraid to take that giant step into a new career, returning to school, purchasing a home, or starting a business. This book will teach them how to get off the couch, continue forward, and take that idea from the drawing board to realization. Make it happen! Forward Motion!

Introduction

Have you ever wondered…

What could have been?

Is this the path your life is supposed to take?

Is there something you should be doing to assure your success and reach your goals?

Is there something more…

Well, if you've had any of these thoughts or similar thoughts, then this book is for you!

This book is for those who know they have more in them than they have been able to give.

For those who dream big *and* see their dreams as possible.

For those who see their dreams as a reality and simply need a plan to propel them into the realm of reality.

For those who have faced roadblock after roadblock, barrier after barrier.

This book is written to show you how to take that dream, idea, thought, wish – something that has been in your head and on your mind, for as long as you can remember – and make it real. Make it happen:

- The dream that through the years, the hard times, and the complicated times… has stayed with you.

- The dream that you've had to push aside to deal with life's everyday needs, life's dilemmas, life's upheavals, life's tribulations… and yet even with all those interferences, your dream is still there. It resurfaces regardless.

- The thing that you want to do more than anything else, the thing you were put on this earth to do, the thing that is in your blood: your calling!

This book will give you the tools to stop procrastinating, to stop pushing those dreams aside, to make those dreams a reality... today!

This book will teach you to dissect all obstacles, put everything into perspective, and to make sure you succeed.

It will help you get on the path to living the life you deserve, today!

This book is written for everyone: Men and women of all ages, educational backgrounds, and economic stages. Whether your dream is purchasing your first home or several homes as an investor, earning a college degree, starting the business you've always wanted, getting into a career, or making the kind of money you've always wanted to make – this book is for you. It will help you find whatever it may be that will allow you to live the life that you know you deserve! The life you know you should have! The time is now! Today! This very minute!

No longer will it be a dream *Deferred*... It will be a dream *Realized!*

Chapter One

Dreams Deferred: Fear & Ambition

Life can be a very satisfying and rewarding journey for those who accomplish their dreams. There is no better satisfaction than to work hard and accomplish what you seek. Whether graduating from college, purchasing a home, starting a business, or reaching a career goal, dreams are made of these accomplishments. However, to some, these dreams are simply that: dreams. Many obstacles exist that prevent the best of us from realizing our dreams. These obstacles come in many forms, and one of the biggest is fear.

Fear can stop you in your tracks. Fear can prevent you from even attempting to achieve success. Fear can immobilize you. Ambition is an opposing force to fear. Ambition slaps fear in the face, punches it in the gut, and kicks its ass! Ambition is what is needed to realize dreams. Do you have ambition? Everyone, at some point in life, has had a dream or vision relating to their life.

The dream could be a good dream or a bad dream. In this book, we're only discussing good dreams. The good dreams usually exhibit something that we would like to have or how we would like something to be. It could be anything from a nice car, boat, home, great career, family, great relationship, financial security, owning a successful business, or anything else.

These dreams can appear in several forms. The dreams can appear as a simple vision or thought that flashes in your head, usually brought on by something else, either visual or verbal. This dream can appear once, occasionally, daily, or even more often. The dream can be a quick flash or an image that causes you to pause from your actions and kind of drift into the dream, a kind of pause that you may not realize you are caught in, but others do. A pause where someone asks you, "Where were you?" or "Are you alright?" The dream can also appear as images while you are sleeping. As a sleeping dream, your subconscious is in control. This type of vision may even surprise sleepers, as they may not have realized what thoughts were in their minds.

Whichever way the dream comes, one thing is for sure: everyone dreams. Those with money and those without, those with education and those without, even those who appear to have everything – everyone dreams of having more or of losing what they have. All it takes to have dreams is exposure, desire, and fear. By exposure I mean just knowing that something else exists different from what you have or are doing. I'm not sure whether someone who is not exposed to a different way, would dream of living differently.

For instance, the children and adults shown on television in underdeveloped countries may dream because they have seen the cameramen and camerawomen, the television network employees and such. They have seen the clothing these people wear, the jewelry they wear, the shoes they wear, the vehicles they travel in, and the equipment they use. Maybe the children and adults in the underdeveloped countries have seen television or magazines at some point in their lives, maybe they have seen the images of how others live. This is exposure that allows them to see that there is a different way of living than the way they live. However, I wonder if those same persons, adults, and children in their natural habitats, not visited by anyone or exposed to any outside images, would dream of a different life. In other words, if the people in the underdeveloped countries only knew of their way of living, would they dream of a different way of living? Some would argue against the idea that exposure leads to desire and dreams, but it holds true in my mind.

Another example of how exposure may have lead to dreams, desires, and wanting a better life is the relationship between the cavemen of prehistoric times and their use of fire without prior knowledge. I would imagine that lightning probably struck an animal, causing it to catch fire and burn to death. A caveman probably saw this and went over to the dead animal and tasted its charred flesh, realizing a better taste, began to find ways to imitate the lightning to recreate the same fire for cooking and heat. This is just a thought, I'm sure there are many other ideas related to the development of the use of fire.

Another ingredient needed for dreams is Desire. Desire can be conscious or sub-conscious. Consciously, a person may desire to have something or to live a better life. Subconsciously, a person's desire may surface as mental images while sleeping. Desire is simply wanting something. Desire can be in the form of hope as well. A person suffering from a sickness or disease may desire a life without the disease or desire a cure being found.

Consciously or subconsciously, fear can also be an ingredient of dreams. Your fear of something happening or not happening can cause you to dream. A person who is afraid of roller coasters may dream of riding the biggest, most treacherous roller coaster ever built. A person dealing with hard times may dream of becoming homeless or losing everything.

Everyone dreams, but what makes us all different is our level of ambition. It is our ambition that gives us the power to make our dreams come true. There are those who see their dreams as just that: dreams. There are people who think that a dream is not meant to come true, that it is simply a dream – a form of entertainment or unknown function that occurs within the human psyche. I disagree! I see a dream as a signal that you or your body desires something or fears something. A dream should be a signal to take action. Your dreams should at least force you to take a look at an issue or situation. After examining the issue, it may not be the right time in your life for you to act on it, but you should at least examine it. It may be something that requires you to put a large plan together before you can spring into the action. This will allow you to execute that dream several years down the line. In fact, your plan can take thirty, forty, or even fifty years to take shape, all while achieving small milestones along the way. Even if your dream is based on the fear of something, it should cause you to do something to prepare for the inevitable or to prevent it. Ultimately, your dream should cause you to take action and make a plan.

    Many plans are detailed and precise. One's retirement plan is usually very detailed with specific goals. Retirement plans can take many years to develop, but a plan is required. The plan is usually based on your dreams of retirement. Where do you see yourself in your retirement? What do you plan on doing when you retire? Anything worth having requires a plan. Regardless of how long or detailed your plan is, if your dreams are important to you, then you must have a plan to achieve them. Think of it this way: your plan is your roadmap. If you are planning to drive to a place that you've never been to before, one of your first steps is to get a map and map it out. In today's world, you may use an online map or your GPS system. However, you're still mapping it out. You don't just get in your car and go. Well, it's the same thing with success. Your dream or vision is a place where you have never been but would like to go. So, you need a plan, a roadmap.

  That leads me back to the last section of this chapter: ambition. There are many people who have dreams of a better life and a better career. However, they do not have the ambition to go after those dreams. Ambition is a very funny thing. Some people are born with it, some people learn it, and some people will just never have it. Don't get me wrong; everyone has certain things they consider obtainable that they will go after or try to make happen. But some of those same people see obstacles and hard work as a sign of something that is not meant to be. Then there are those who fear failure and won't even try. Can you believe that? I have met a lot of people like that in my life and it amazes me. How can someone think that way? Life itself, our mere existence, is made up of and from difficult, risky decisions. How can people expect to enjoy or have fulfilling lives if they are not willing to try?

Where would we be if Dr. Martin Luther King Jr. had decided, "I'm not getting involved with these race issues because it's too dangerous, it's going to take too long, or it's going to be too difficult"? What if Abraham Lincoln had decided, "I'm not tackling this slavery issue – it's too dangerous, it's going to make enemies, or it's going to be too difficult"? What if our parents from Jamaica, Panama, India, Ireland, China, the Dominican Republic, and other countries decided that they were just going to settle with where God has placed them in life? What if they decided not to try to get a better life for their family and the future generations of their families? Where would they be today? Where would you be today? Black, white, or otherwise, where would we be today if these people had not tried? What I'm trying to show you is that almost everything that exists today does so because someone dreamed of it, they planned to achieve it, and they had the ambition needed to make it happen.

    One thing I've learned to deal with is that many people are content with what they have and what they will never have. Is there anything wrong with that? Probably not, but why settle when you can have anything you want? This world is setup in a way that if you try hard enough and make the right moves, you can pretty much get anything you want out of life. If you want to be a millionaire, there are steps you can and need to take to become one. If you want to become a professional athlete, there are steps you can take to obtain that position. Nothing is guaranteed, but if you don't try, if you don't give your dreams everything you have, if you don't possess the ambition, then there is no chance that you will ever achieve your dreams. No chance! Aren't your dreams worth spending your entire life trying to accomplish? Mine are! But you'd be surprised how many people do not feel this way.

I've heard that the fact that everyone doesn't think or feel this way, balances things out. Basically, the premise explains that there has to be someone to do the lower-level work. If everyone had these big plans and dreams, no one would be willing to do the lower-level work. I disagree with this. I feel that there is a starting point for everyone. Many newly employed people should be willing to do lower-level work and then work their way up to the higher-level work, gaining knowledge and experience along the way to the top or on the way to owning their own business. This lower-level work should be seen as a stepping stone.

Then you have those who get into this lower-level work and then become stagnant. They feel they cannot achieve more or become comfortable with what they have and do not want to continue in a forward motion. The funny thing is that it'll be those same people who complain about things to no end. Those same people will blame someone else or the government for everything from the lack of opportunity, to overtaxing them, to their living conditions, etc. They will never see that opportunities exist for everyone. What you have and where you are is based on how hard you are willing to work to get what you want. If you are only willing to take the easy road, the comfortable road, if you are not willing to push yourself, sacrifice, get dirty, work long hours, and get little sleep, then how can you expect to achieve the riches of life? No one is going to give success to you! If you want it, go for it! Don't shy away from hard work.

  It amazes me how so many people live in this country for years, some in the same communities for their whole lives, as spectators. They complain when the neighborhood changes, they complain when the local stores are bought out, they complain when new buildings go up, but they are just spectators. They just sit back, watching life change and pass them by from the sidelines. They don't make any moves to jump in. As you know, what usually ends up happening is that people from other countries come into this country and buy buildings or businesses. Many don't even speak the English language well, but they can come to the United States and, based on ambition and determination, start a business, buy a home, go to college, and succeed. Sure the government may help them, but there is also help available for everyone, in the form of minority assistance, low-income assistance, academic-based assistance, etc. You are supposed to take advantage of whatever is out there, no matter how much is available for you compared to how much is available for someone else. Who cares? Take what you can and run with it! If you have to take a year to do research, make phone calls, and write letters to find out what's available, then do it. It's all part of the process. At least you're doing something to work on your dream, and you're that much closer.

Don't get me wrong; there is nothing wrong with being content with what you have. I guess. Mediocrity is alright for some people, but I believe that life is all about progression and forward motion. My parents wanted me to achieve more than they did, and

I have. I want my children to achieve more than I have, and they will. That is how life should be: Forward Motion!

Here are some quotes that have kept me motivated throughout the years:

- Live like you were dying.
  Tim McGraw

- Go confidently in the direction of your dreams. Live the life you have imagined.
  Henry David Thoreau

- Go for it now. The future is promised to no one.
  Wayne Dyer

- Dream as if you'll live forever. Live as if you'll die today.
  James Dean

- When I stand before God at the end of my life, I would hope that I would not have a single bit of talent left, and could say, I used everything you gave me.
  Erma Bombeck

- Let your life mean something. Become an inspiration to others so they may try to do more and to become more than they are today.
  Thomas D. Willhite

- Strategy is strength.
Unknown Author

- I have learned that courage was not the absence of fear, but the triumph over it. The brave man is not he who does not feel afraid, but he who conquers that fear.
Nelson Mandela

Chapter Two

Spouses, Partners, & Family

This is a tricky area. For many, families are their support system. Many have families that will understand their goals and dreams. You may have a family that will do everything it can to support and help you reach your goal. Your family members may help open doors for you, provide the push you need, and be your cheering section. However, this is not always the case.

Having a spouse, partner, or family can create situations that could take you off track… if you let them. Family can be one of the biggest issues hindering your success. This hindrance can come in the form of family members who don't understand your dream or goal, who believe in going through life the way they have. That "way" may not include college, owning your own business, or pursuing what they conceive to be a non-traditional career choice. They may have gone through life simply working for someone else, being a loyal employee, saving for and purchasing a home, providing sufficiently for their family, and working until retirement age. That may be their idea of success: following the norm. This may be what they expect from you as well. But you have your own dreams and goals.

The hindrance could also be in the form of jealousy. Family may not like the fact that you want something more, better, or different than what they had or provided. Your desire for more may be viewed as though you feel that they were not successful or successful enough. Usually, this jealousy will present itself in the form of negative comments, irrational questions, and bold ambiguous statements. You will recognize it when you see or hear it.

There is a passive type of hindrance that can also exist and is usually associated with a spouse, children, or taking care of family members. In this situation, it is not anyone's fault nor is it that anyone is doing anything on purpose to stop you, but it can be the obligation alone that may slow you down or even cause you to put off or stop chasing your dream. Sometimes, merely having the obligation and responsibility of taking care of others will create barriers or roadblocks in your mind. The obstacle or roadblock could be financial, the lack of time to pursue your goals, or the fear of risking everyone's well being.

Whatever the case, having or planning a family can be seen as a hindrance. These issues should not be seen as a hindrance. In fact, you have several choices in dealing with these family issues. You can simply ignore them. You can continue to be around family members who do not understand your goals or are jealous of your dreams and simply ignore them. You can also limit your exposure to these family members. By not being around them, you will not hear the negative comments or have to deal with the ridiculous questions.

Another option is to take the time to explain your dreams and goals, attempting to bring clarity and understanding to the forefront. This could mean explaining to family elders how times have changed and how you don't see limits or have different aspirations than they had. This can lead to increased animosity from these family members directed at you and your dreams. The conflict created through openly and verbally challenging their ways of thinking and living may not be worth it.

The final option is to use all possible hindrances as challenges that make you stronger and more determined. When a family elder tells you that you should be happy with what you have or that you should not try to be better than anyone else, you can just smile and keep on moving. All the while, in your mind, you are thinking of how good you will feel when your successes become apparent. You will use their negative comments and questions as strength, as fire in your belly, and as a weapon in your success arsenal. This attention is a positive sign that you are going against the grain and stepping outside the box to follow your dreams.

This also holds true for the passive hindrance associated with having family obligations and responsibility. Use it as strength, as why it is even more important that you succeed. If this passive hindrance includes children, find strength in knowing that you are showing them that anything they want in life is possible. Think of the example you are setting for them. Think of the man or woman that your spouse or partner has, expects, or wants. Think of how proud your partner and family are going to be, not only of you and your successes but because they were correct in what they saw in you.

    Now don't get me wrong, not everyone will have to deal with these issues; however, if you do, find strength in it. Know that you can make your dreams come true if you have a family or are planning a family. It may be a juggling act, but remember, nothing can stand in your way, not even family. You will just have to become a juggler; you have no choice. See it as one obstacle, not a stop, just an obstacle. Remember that. It is important that you understand that. You must continue in a Forward Motion!

Chapter Three

Friends and the Company We Keep

This chapter is what I like to call the "Oops factor." In life, there are a lot of things that happen that are not in our control. Some of these things end up being negative occurrences that can and do change the course of our lives. Many times, these negative occurrences can involve or are the result of friends and the company we keep. That being said, it is important to remember to choose your friends and the company you keep carefully.

If you are a very ambitious, goal orientated, success-driven person, then you should spend your time with the same type of people. People with similar drive and ambition tend to think alike, have the same interest, and see life the same way. This is important because when it comes to taking silly risks and doing things that don't make sense, you'll be on the same page. If you are this sort of person, then your focus is probably on your future and your success. You probably won't want to be out getting high, drinking, or hanging out on street corners. As an even better option, associate yourself with those whom you deem successful – the types of people who have already reached the level that you want to reach. This association means finding a way to make a continuous connection with a respected or knowledgeable family member, a successful businessman or businesswoman, a successful colleague, a learned professor, homeowners, real estate investors, etc. Talk to these people, introduce yourself, attend functions where such people frequent, and join specific associations or organizations. Your goal is to get in on their conversations, gain insight into what they do, what they are doing, what they plan to do. You will be surprised how many successful people are willing to talk to you, share their knowledge, give you suggestions, and take you under their wing. These are known as Type-A people and usually are associated with a strong will and determination to succeed. Type-A people are known to enjoy giving advice and sharing their knowledge. This association does not have to be a formal situation. It can begin with an email, a letter, a text, and even attending a family function to make that connection. The key is to make that connection! To reach out!

I know several individuals who were focused on success, had a good head on their shoulders, and had a plan for their lives. Unfortunately, their lives were destroyed by hanging with the wrong crowd. Now, I'm not blaming their friends for getting them into trouble – not at all. The bottom line is that the individuals chose to hang out with the wrong crowd. The individuals were aware of their friend's lifestyle but still chose to hang out with them, as they have done many times in the past. It just so happens that their luck ran out. They ended up being in the wrong place at the wrong time. Many ended up with criminal records – or worse, dead. Had they stayed home or did something else that night, the results may have been different. Their lives could have been different.

I've found myself in similar situations several times in my youth. It was a learning process. There were several times in my youth that my life could have taken a wrong turn. And when I look back, I remember saying on some occasions, "Why am I doing this? I shouldn't be doing this!" or "I hope I don't regret this." Even with all my questions, I continued to go along with the situation, mostly because I didn't want to be ridiculed by the guys. I guess I was lucky though, because I never got into any trouble, although there were a few very close calls. The funny thing is that I knew I was different - not better or smarter, just different. I had a different outlook on life than they did. I knew that I was just hanging out and having fun for the night. I had serious plans for my life. However, I believe that some of those guys wished that they could've stopped time and lived in that particular youthful, carefree moment, forever. I knew that I had a future and I was excited about my future. I knew that I was going to college, I knew that I'd someday have a career and maybe even own a business or two. In fact, my dreams were grandiose, always.

    One particular incident that stays at the forefront of my mind occurred on a hot summer day during my high school years.

The guys I hung out with on this particular day included several friends of friends who I didn't know. I wasn't driving yet, but one of the guys we were with, one of the friends of a friend, was pretty high in the drug game, even though he was our age. He would rent cars for weeks at a time because he was too important to take the train and bus to high school like the rest of us. This was in the days when rental cars had license plates that started with the letter Z. On this day, during summer break, we attended an event at a local high school. It was five African American males inside of a shiny, brand new, late model, rental car, with the music blasting, and blazing through the streets on our way to this event.

    We got there, parked in front of the school and went to the school's gym where the event was being held. During this event, the friend of a friend who drove us to the event, who we'll call Greg, got into some "beef" with another guy over a girl. The guy challenged Greg to a hand-to-hand fight. The fight started in the school's gym. However, each party mutually agreed to take it outside. At this point, everyone's interest shifted from the event to this "beef". Everyone assembled outside to watch this fight. The fight began on one side of a very busy, four-lane, median-divided, two-way street. Things started out fair and Greg was getting the best of his challenger; he was winning the fight. The challenger's boys didn't like this, so they began jumping in with canes, striking Greg and causing his head to bleed. Some of the guys in our group also jumped in, but most of us didn't because we didn't know Greg enough to fight an unknown fight with him. What we did instead was to hold back as many of the other guys who wanted to jump in, as we could.

During this altercation, while holding several guys back, being the very observant person I was even back then, I began looking around. I noticed an "unmarked" (police car) parked at the corner about a block away. I could see the images of at least three people in the car. I immediately yelled out "Cops! Yo, the cops are up the block watching us!" Everything stopped, everyone ran.

We all jumped back into Greg's shiny rental, sped off, and noticed that the unmarked never moved. Greg was pissed because he was winning the fight and then the other guy's boys jumped in. He kept saying, "It was supposed to be a fair one!", as he navigated the back streets and held his bleeding head. We ended up at his house, in his bedroom, where he cleaned his wounds and changed out of his bloodstained clothes.

Still angry at the situation, Greg said, "I know where they hang-out! This shit ain't over!" He kept saying repeatedly, "This shit ain't over!" Greg dropped to the ground and reached under his bed, pulling out a black duffle bag. In the bag were guns. Not the type you see on TV. These were some beat-up looking guns. He reached into the bag and pulled out a sawed-off shotgun. It was obvious that the barrel and the shoulder stock were sawed off by hand. In fact, because the shoulder stock was sawed off, it was wrapped in black electrical tape. He yelled out, "I got something for them; it's time to pull out the shotty!" He pumped the shotgun once and stated, "We're going back out!" No one grabbed any of the other guns from the bag, and I'm not sure why. I don't know if it was because it was his beef or because the guys I hung out with weren't street guys who dealt with guns.

Anyway, we jumped back into the shiny rental, he put the "shotty" in the trunk of the car, and we headed back out. Greg was still driving, and I was in the back seat behind the passenger seat. So here we were driving around looking for these guys. This time instead of speeding around like we normally did, we drove very slowly, creeping. About 15-20 minutes in, we heard a yelp and saw flashing lights behind us. My heart stopped as I turned my head and saw the same unmarked that I had seen at the high school. We all mumbled, "Oh shit!!!" Greg told us to calm down, not to panic, and to let him do all the talking.

Greg pulled over, and three plainclothes officers got out of the unmarked and approached the car. If the police checked the trunk, we were done. I was done. One of the officers went to Greg and began asking him questions; the second officer went to the front passenger side and began asking questions; the third officer went to the rear of the vehicle and watched the back seat passengers. Luckily, they didn't order us out of the car, they didn't look in the trunk, and they let us go. We immediately went back to Greg's house, he put the "shotty" back in his room, and we had him drive us back to our neighborhood. What might have happened if that turned out differently? What kind of future would I have had? I knew what Greg was into; everyone knew. Yet we still hung out with him through several other similar incidents where the "shotty" made an appearance.

In fact, after several more very narrow escapes and the progression of my education, my boys saw less and less of me. When we did hang out, I realized that the conversations we had were senseless. I realized that I wasn't interested in the same things that they were interested in. I realized that my friends did not want to talk about the things that interested me. We grew apart. On several occasions I recall talking about wanting to be successful, to travel, to have a big house, a boat, and a helicopter. My boys thought I was crazy; they didn't understand why I was talking about these things, why I was dreaming so crazy, why I was acting like I was better than them. They began to ask me, "Yo, what's up? You don't hang out with us anymore!" It was true. I began to shy away from my boys. Mainly because I realized that the risk I was taking was not worth it. The fact that we had very different ways of thinking and looking at life made me realize that I did not want to end up where they were likely to end up, at least not on purpose. I knew that I had to follow my dreams, and part of that meant staying steadfast and focused. I had my own plans for my life, and as I got older and exposed to more of life, my dreams became bigger and clearer. I wanted success bad; I could taste it. Nothing and no one was going to stand in my way. Especially not me! Forward Motion!

Chapter Four

Drugs, Alcohol, and Other Vices

Now here's a show stopper! We all know that alcohol in moderation is OK, but drugs, on the other hand, are not acceptable. The problem with these vices is that they can make you forget your plans and just indulge in the moment. That one moment can destroy your life. Change the course of events.

Without getting into specifics, I can say that in my youth, I've been in uncomfortable, unsafe, unhealthy, and foolish situations involving these vices. Some of you can probably say the same. What kept me from falling and floundering in that life were several factors. When I was younger, it was my mother. Not that she was with me in the streets or anything like that, but my mother was a very verbal person. Anyone who knew her would tell you that. Growing up and being raised in Jamaica, Queens, New York, my mother would always speak to my sister and me in attempts to protect us from the unknown. Some would call it preaching, prophesying, or educating. She had her fears, as all parents do, about her children growing up in a tough neighborhood. My mother would repeatedly tell my sister and me about the fears and the evils that exist in the world. She professed her expectations of us and told us what and who to avoid. My mother ran scenarios and worked through the solutions with us. She was very blunt in her conversations and the way she broke things down for us. When I found myself in situations involving drugs and alcohol, I could see her face, the fear in it, and I could hear her voice. I knew the disappointment that would follow if I ended up hurt, arrested – or worst, dead.

    Now don't get me wrong: This imagery didn't stop me, as is evident from the story in the last chapter. However, it made me aware of what I was doing. It allowed me to set limits and to look for signs to know when to stop and when to "bounce." What's important is that I did not let it become *me*. I did not allow it to take over my life. That leads me to the second factor that prevented me from floundering in drugs and alcohol – myself. As I became older, I became wiser. My dreams and goals would not let me fall to the obvious bait! I knew that if I was going to succeed and accomplish my dreams, there was no place for anything that warped my mind, prevented me from thinking, or caused me to live in the moment so much that I'd forget my future. I wanted no part of that. Nothing was going to stop me, especially not drugs or alcohol, especially not me.

I saw several friends get stuck in this life, lose their jobs, become alcoholics, addicts, and waste away to nothing. Then there were those who learned to master it. They lived regular lives and had alcohol and drugs as a "side-job." As a result, they were stuck in a life where they were slaves to these vices. Whether they indulged in excess every day, every night, or every weekend, they couldn't shake it. Their lack of control got to the point where I realized and asked myself, "why even do it?" I was a young, strong, healthy young man with my whole life ahead of me. Am I going to be so dependent on a substance that I can't take control and stop? Absolutely not! I chose me, my life, and success!

The lesson here is, get a hold of your life. Assess your vices and make sure that they don't have control over you – whatever that vice may be. It may be marijuana, drugs, alcohol, patronizing prostitutes, gambling, or anything else that takes you away from focusing on your dream. It is probably that thing in your life that brings confusion, stress, or strife into your life. The issue that a family member, wife, girlfriend, boyfriend, boss, teacher, or professor sees the signs of and may have even spoken to you about. The thing that you know makes you late for work, school, or appointments. The issue that has caused you to lose weight, gain weight, or look bad. Or maybe you have control of it and have mastered it. Maybe no one knows, no one sees the signs, and no one suspects. But you know, you see the signs, and you know how it's affecting you. You must remember that anything that takes you off your game, off your 100%, can be your downfall. Do not let a vice control your life. *You* are in control of your life. Don't waste energy hiding the issue, lying to people, making excuses, and not accomplishing a thing.

What could the positive side of these vices be? Realistically, there are none. Obviously, you are a person with goals, dreams, and aspirations; otherwise, you wouldn't be reading this book. You have it in you, and you know this. Straighten up, fix yourself, whatever that means to your situation, whatever that takes in your situation. Learn from your errors. You are in control of your destiny. Forward Motion!

Chapter Five

Education

This is one of my favorite areas. I've always believed in the saying that knowledge is power! In fact, I have that imprinted on my high school graduation ring. That's how long I've been on my quest to achieve my dreams.

Education is the key to success. What I mean by that is education is one of the keys that can open the door to success. There are many ingredients to success, and education is just one of them. However, it is important to understand that because a person has an education, does not mean that he or she will be successful. It is also important to understand that although education is the key to success, it is not an absolute ingredient. Meaning that to be successful, one does not necessarily have to have an education. Education can and usually helps on the road to success, but success can be achieved without education. It is relative to what success means to you. If you'd like to be a successful doctor, then of course education is a key. However, if your dream is to be a successful athlete or singer, for example, then education is not as much a key to your success, but it can help you develop into a person with a clearer outlook on life.

From my experiences, those who have an education beyond high school usually hold a specific mindset. They understand that education is not only beneficial in their quest, but it also provides insight into life. Learning opens the mind, and with an open mind comes understanding and ideas. Education can change a person. It can create a person who sees! When I say "see," I mean a person with clear vision. A person who sees into the future – the possibilities, the options, the obstacles, and the path forward. Education is empowering and uplifting. It can provide just the right amount of aggression, boldness, confidence, determination, and strength to know that anything you want is possible. You will understand that.

Another benefit of education is that with every higher level one achieves, the positioning in the company, salary, income, and earning potential should increase as well. Of course, there is no guarantee, but it is expected. Of course, this doesn't apply to all areas of success. If you are a corporate executive and you currently have a bachelors degree, and you decide to return to school to obtain a master's degree, part of that decision is usually the fact that you will earn more money. You'd expect the money to come either immediately upon the completion of the degree or once you obtain a higher position based on the qualifications that your new advanced degree affords you. There are many careers and professions where education and hard work are the keys to success. On the same note, there are many careers where education does not play a role.

However, what I want to discuss in this chapter is high school education and the decision to attend college. I'm hoping that a lot of my readers are the youth of this country. I'd like the messages contained in this book to reach the younger generation. One of the messages is that you need an education. For those of you who are considering dropping out of school, who currently do not attend school, or who are not taking school seriously, this message is for you. So, listen up! Go to school! If you cannot complete the basic requirements that this country has in place, then what are you doing? Many of today's youth believe that they do not have to conform to the standards of society. They honestly feel that they can achieve their goals without any education. I've talked with many young people who no longer go to school or are dropouts, and who say to me, "Go to school? Why? Because *they* say so? Why should I have to do what *they* say? I'm doing me. There's nothing for me there." Let me tell you, this is a problem. A big problem.

Is it laziness, or are these young people just doing what they are being allowed to get away with? Either way, it's not a good thing. Our youth need an education. Where are these kid's parents? I don't want to get into that right now because people don't like to hear my views on that. I'll just say that those parents lost those kids a long time ago. Those kids have been on their own, making their own decisions for a long time now. Their parents can't tell them anything. You can pretty much say, "The streets got those kids." It's sad but very true. Many of those kids have so much potential, but they are lost. Some of them are just off track, some are rebelling, and some of them are testing the waters because you know the grass always looks greener on the other side of the fence. Unfortunately, many of them will get in trouble, one way or another, before they realize what they should have done. For many, by the time they realize, start to see the truth, or just wake up, they'll have marks against them that, in some cases, will make it impossible for them to proceed in the direction that they know they should have been following the whole time.

  That's why education so important, especially for those who are somewhere in the middle of one of the situations I've described. Stop what you're doing and get back on track. Understand that there is no fast or easy way to make it and especially understand this: What you may see out there, and the example of people who have "made it" in your eyes are one of two things. They either exist on borrowed time, which will lead to arrest or death, or they are the very rare exceptions. The rappers who have made it big, the drug dealers, and the pimps that have appeared to have made it big, are not really what they seem. They are few and far between.

Look at it this way, rather than buck the system, use the system. You see doctors, lawyers, and CEO's living in these fancy homes, with expensive cars, and lavish lifestyles? Is that what you want? Then make it happen, the sure and definite way. Study hard and finish high school, then go to college, and then go to graduate school, law school, or medical school. That is the same path that most of these legitimate people have taken to achieve what they have obtained. Once you've done all that, who can deny you? If you've worked your ass off and have achieved the required education, who can deny you? When you walk into a hospital with your medical degree and apply for a job, or you walk into a law office with your law degree, who can deny you? You may not start at the level or in the position that you wanted, but you're now a doctor or a lawyer; who can deny you? It's only a matter of time.

Once you get your foot in the door, then you can show them what you're made of, and work your way up to where you want to be. All the riches will follow. But none of this will happen if you don't make the effort to go to school. There is always a way!

For those of you who are saying that you can't afford college, I say this: If you're in high school, "Bust that shit out!" Work your ass off in high school. Limit and control the hanging out and partying. You have your whole life to do that. Study as hard as you can, get the best grades you possibly can, ace the SAT's, and try to get a scholarship.

Another option is to get a job. Many students are forced to work while they are in school. Some students even work full time and attend school full time. If you're attending a college that is somewhat affordable, living at home, or if you're receiving partial financial aid or scholarships, working to supplement the tuition is an option. This is a tough situation, but it can be done. It is definitely not impossible. Nothing should be at this point if you want it bad enough. I worked full time while obtaining my bachelor's degree and my graduate degrees, and I know others who have as well. It requires focus and even greater determination because there will be many nights that you'll go without sleep. It is probably the most difficult way to go to school, but your determination to reach your goal will not let anything stop you from achieving and reaching it. Forward Motion!

Chapter Six

Running Solo

Let me start by explaining what I mean by "Running Solo." When I use this term, I'm referring to being willing to stand alone, step out from the crowd, go at it when everyone else is against you, and pushing forward without any support – even in the face of opposition.

One thing I've learned is that people dance to their own beat. That's what makes us all different. There are those who live and will die for success – it burns in their souls. In psychology, this is called having a Type A personality. Then there are those who do not care at all about attaining a certain level of success. They move and operate in a very relaxed, laid back manner. This is known as a Type B personality. So that you know where I stand, both personalities are fine with me. There was a time in my life when I could not understand anything but a Type A personality. I now believe and understand the saying "to each his own."

Anyway, back to what I was saying: You have to be willing to go at it alone. If you have a support system, then that's great. However, understand that even without that support system, you must succeed. Most people usually have someone in their corner, someone who has their back. But understand that there are different kinds of support. There are those who will simply listen to your idea and agree, there are those who will listen and give their honest opinion, and then there are those who will listen, inquire, follow-up, and even help. The latter is the kind of support that will motivate you and help you when you're having doubts or falling into a rut. There is nothing better than that kind of support. Unfortunately, it doesn't always happen.

Nonetheless, you have to be able to progress with or without support. You have to be able to cast all the naysayers to the side. You have to be able to go at it alone – solo. There will be times when you need a push, someone to kick you in your ass or throw you out of bed. You may not have that. You still have to get up, to find the motivation, the power, and the strength, to get moving even when you don't want to. Always remember: Every step is positive. The smallest baby step is still a step. Even a step backward should be seen as a positive, learning step. A step backward is usually due to an oversight, an unforeseen occurrence or situation, a mistake, or an error. Errors and mistakes are meant to be learning tools. They are supposed to highlight and cause you to evaluate the situation to find out what you did wrong, what you failed to do, or what you overlooked. A backward step should be used as a springboard of sorts to move you even further forward onto the next step. Sometimes you also need to take a step backward to see what you've accomplished and where you're heading. A backward step is sometimes needed to evaluate the direction or progress of your plan. It can serve as a check and balance system for your plan.

    The bottom line is that you need to be prepared to "run solo." Relying on other people will only hold you back and can take you off track. There is nothing worse than a talented person who feels that he or she cannot move forward without the acknowledgment or support of other people. I know this because I have been there a few times in my life. It's a very strange situation. There have been times where I've felt that because no one was interested in my ideas or no one asked me about them, then the ideas were insignificant and not worth pursuing. But they were! They were significant to me! And I've learned that I do not need anyone to validate them. If they are my dreams, visions, and ambitions, then they are important!

I have learned that to be successful, you need not be concerned with what anyone else thinks. You have to be your own motivation. You have to be your own cheering section. And never – I mean never – let the lack of enthusiasm or the lack of support ever slow you down or cause you to doubt or question your dreams or what you are doing to accomplish them. As they say, "You are the Captain of your ship."

I also want to address another very specific situation I've found myself in. That situation is the feeling that you cannot do it alone. When I say "alone," I mean without a partner, not necessarily support, but without another person taking the journey along with you. There have been times in my life where I've felt that once I explain my idea and plan to someone, they should see how great the idea is and jump right in. During those times, the fact that this enthusiasm was not present has caused me to stop. The stop was to analyze not only the idea or plan but also the friendship or relationship that I was in with that person. I was taking their lack of enthusiasm personally. Analyzing the plan or idea was a good thing, but analyzing the friendship or relationship was ridiculous.

If it is my idea, my plan, then I should be prepared – in fact, expect – to do it alone. I should not question the person's loyalty or friendship if they do not jump in with me. I just finished explaining that everyone has their own way of thinking. Do not let the fact that you have to do it alone scare you away from pursuing your dreams and doing what has to be done to accomplish them.

So, remember: Be prepared to run solo! Forward Motion!

Chapter Seven

Don't Sweat the Small Thinking.

Leveling Significance

The title of this chapter can be misleading and misunderstood. In this chapter, when I refer to small thinking, I am not referring to thinking small in the business sense. I'm referring to being obsessed or preoccupied with the small things that take energy away from where your focus should be directed.

Too many people waste enormous amounts of energy on factors that are insignificant to their success and wellbeing. Some of these things may not be small things, but in comparison to the significance of the plans, goals, and dreams that are theirs, such things are small. Small in the sense of importance. Being a success, achieving your goals, and making your dreams come true are difficult enough tasks. Therefore, why waste so much energy on insignificant things or people who are insignificant to your success?

That may sound harsh, but in life there should be family, close friends, and loved ones who provide significance in your life one way or another; then, there are regular friends and acquaintances. These acquaintances are people you may work with or deal with in one way or another, who have no real significance in your life. When I say that they have no significance, I do not mean that they are not nice people, good people, or important to their own or someone else's life. What I mean is that in the overall outlook of your life and your life's plans, they aren't at the same level in your life as close friends, family, and loved ones. You must be able to distinguish between the different relationship levels of the people in your life. By understanding these levels, you can better interact with these people and avoid the negative aspects of wasted energy.

This energy that I refer to usually comes in the form of concern with what that person has, is doing, or gets away with. Do you know people like this? They are always concerned about other people, always talking about what other people have or are getting away with. So many people focus on this in their lives. The attitude is, "Hey, how come he/she got that or gets to do that, and I don't?" This is so aggravating, and it is difficult for me to be around people like this. It drives me crazy! I can't reiterate enough about how important it is that you do not get caught up in this mentality. There is no time for this; it will drain you and make you a bitter person. I've seen many lose focus on what should be important, instead focusing on insignificant matters.

There is nepotism, favoritism, racism, reverse racism, and general ass-kissing that has and will always exist. In most cases, there is very little that can be done to offset or eliminate these things without devoting excessive amounts of your most needed and vital energy. You must be the person who is not concerned with what others are doing or getting, besides exploring to see how you can benefit or better your position by duplicating an acceptable action or becoming enlightened about a program or option that you did not realize existed or hadn't explored.

    I have worked with people who were able to get away with many things that others couldn't. Not necessarily criminal things, just simple overlooked behavior and certain freedoms not afforded to others. Now I could've been one of several people with regard to this. I could've been the one who complained that this person gets to do this, how come I don't. I could've been the person who said, "If he or she can do it, so can I." This is not always a bad option, but it can cause a lot of energy to be expelled fighting your cause and your position. I could also have been the one who said, "Good for him/her! When it is my turn, I'm going to take full advantage." The latter mindset is why I continue forward with my grind, my dreams, and my goals. Focusing on another's actions is a waste of my time. My energy, especially as I get older and my energy reduces, is too important to squander. It slows the pace, stops the forward motion, and can even create reverse motion.

None of these outcomes are beneficial to the progress needed to succeed.

Stay focused on your dreams and goals. There is no time for insignificant stray issues to cloud your focus and your judgment. Stay focused! Forward Motion!

Chapter Eight

Motivation – Find Yours

Motivation is huge! Along with ambition, one must have the motivation to put together the plan, to execute the plan, and to make one's dreams and goals a reality. The ambition comes from the dream and the desire to achieve something great, but the motivation comes from the power within. Motivation is the coal or wood that keeps the fire in your gut burning. Motivation is the inner strength that allows you to see every obstacle, barrier, and set-back as a stepping stone and learning point along the journey to greatness. It is the motivation that will not let you stop, not let you give up. You must *find* motivation in order to succeed. You must *have* motivation in order to succeed.

There are those who want something, want to be great, want to be successful, but simply do not have the motivation to carry out the plan or take the necessary actions to achieve those goals and dreams. Many people become comfortable in a certain way of life that they currently find themselves in, whether it is the comfort of living at home with mom and dad, the ease and comfort associated with a job where they know they can do better, or neglecting to attend college, knowing it is a necessary step to the success they desire. Unfortunately, many lack the motivation to get up, make a move, and move forward. Many people are stuck – in their minds.

A hypothetical example of motivation comes to mind in the form of a basketball player on a high school team, or any team for that matter - a young man of, say, 15 years old. The youngster wants to be a great player, to make the team, to be a vital player on the team, to get noticed by peers, the coaches, the scouts, to get recruited to a great college team, and then into the into the NBA. While at home he practices his shots, the drills, and the plays, knowing that it is his performance that will get him noticed. During the next game his performance is not what he wants it to be. He misses several shots, his positioning is off during the execution of a few plays, and he misses a game-changing free throw. He is down in the dumps and feeling responsible for letting his team down. Now, this player may still have the ambition to be a great player and make it to the NBA, but does he have the motivation to overcome his disappointment, others' disappointment in him? To understand the issues that need fixing, set a plan to fix them, and to execute the plan to greatness? Will he continue in a Forward Motion, or will he stop?

    I will use a real-life example by describing my background, my path, and my journey to the point where I am today. I grew up in Jamaica, Queens, New York, with two immigrant parents, who came to this country from Panama and became citizens. My mother came to the United States in the 1960s and originally lived in an apartment with family while my father served in the U.S. Army. My mother eventually rented an apartment in Kew Gardens, New York, and when my father returned from the military, they used the GI Bill and their savings to purchase a home in Jamaica, Queens. Although I was born while living at the apartment in Kew

Gardens and later lived in a house in Jamaica, Queens, my sister was born into the home in Jamaica, Queens.

We were both fortunate enough to attend an African-American private school based in St. Albans, Queens, named Lakeview Educational Institute. The school was heavily focused on including the African-American facts of the U.S. history. We learned cursive writing, participated in seasonal plays and performances, and were required to learn about African-American heroes like Crispus Attucks, Mary Mcleod-Bethune, Benjamin Banneker, and many more. In fact, there were so many heroes that their pictures, with a short brief on their contributions, were hung on the walls near the ceiling, around the entire interior perimeter of the main hallway in the school. After graduating from Lakeview in the sixth grade, my parents sent me to a private Jewish junior high school named Oakdale, located in Bayside, Queens, NY. This was big for me because I now had to take two buses to school. The first bus ran along what was then New York Boulevard to Jamaica Avenue. Then I had to walk approximately five blocks along

Jamaica Avenue to 169th Street, where I took another bus to Bayside, Queens. This was big because although I was still going to a private school, I would now be interacting with public school kids. The walk along Jamaica Avenue was always filled with adventure and thrilling sights. Kids would get robbed of their sneakers, coats, jewelry, Cazal glasses, and of course money – right in front of me. In fact, it also happened on the bus rides to Jamaica Avenue and Bayside. The bus to Bayside, Queens had students going to Francis Lewis High School, St. Francis Prep, Bayside High School, and Cardozo High School. Drinking, smoking, fighting, and robberies were daily occurrences from the older high school students on the bus. I avoided these occurrences at this age.

High school was an entirely different animal. My parents wanted me to continue my private school education through high school. That was not my plan. I had enough of the sheltered life and told my parents that I wanted to mix with regular kids and did not want to continue in this sheltered way. My mother fought with me on the issue for a while, but eventually told me I could go to public school if I were accepted into one of the specialized schools in the city. At that time, you had to take a single specialized school exam where your score would determine whether you could attend either Stuyvesant High School, Bronx High School of Science, or Brooklyn Technical High School. I also took the exam for Aviation High School because I was fascinated with airplanes. I was accepted into both Brooklyn Technical High School and Aviation High School. I chose Aviation High School and was determined to follow my youthful dream of becoming a pilot.

My high school years were the interesting years; I got involved with girls, experimented with alcohol, and became a man. I say that I became a man because it was at this time, that I began to think for myself. I began to look around me, at the people I was with, my parents, their lives, my community, and my circumstances. During this time, I began to realize that I was the one person who controlled my life and its outcome. My destiny was in my hands. It was during my high school years that I realized

I had to be motivated and determined in order to succeed. I realized that I had to break away from the average and go for the above average, the exceptional. It was during these years that I first heard about setting up one's life in five-year increments, five-year goals. I set five-year goals for every five years for the rest of my life. Once I set the goals, I knew I had to change things in my life in order to reach these goals. Setting the goals forced me to see that I had to change.

It was this change that stirred the motivation inside of me. It turned me into a motivated, determined, and focused individual. This motivation to succeed caused me to always have a job, work harder at whatever job I had, and continue to push, and push, and push some more until whatever the dream or goal I had at the time was accomplished. After high school, I chose to pursue college instead of a career in the aviation field. Remember, when I said dreams and goals change – well that is the first example. I decided to obtain student loans to go to college on Long Island to pursue my bachelor's degree. I worked full time in many different jobs while in college. At one point, I was making the daily commute all the way to Manhattan, in my first car, a 1978 Oldsmobile 98 that I bought for $900 at a police auction. The car was a theft recovery that had a busted ignition and no wheels. People laughed at me when I had the car towed home, and it sat there on the ground with no wheels, but I made it work. I was in full motivation mode. I worked hard, saved all I could, and bought wheels and tires and got that car on the road. I would arrive in Manhattan three hours before my shift started, double park in an area where street parking was permitted after a certain hour and overnight, and study while waiting for a parking space to become available.

Once I graduated with my bachelor's degree in computer engineering technology, I began working in the computer and electronics field. I quickly realized that this decision was leading me to a life where I would have to work for the next 40 years until I was 65 years old before I could retire. A friend of mine that I hadn't seen since high school stopped by my house one evening and told me he had stopped going to college and joined the police department a few years back. I was shocked and immediately asked him about our dreams to get college degrees. He broke things down for me. He explained to me that I would have to work for at least the next 40 years to be able to retire, while he could retire in 20 years and receive half of his final salary in the form of a pension for the rest of his life. He further explained that he was in the position to get the police department to pay for his undergraduate, graduate, and even law school education through scholarships, if he chose. He detailed the free medical insurance and the right to carry a firearm to protect himself and his family for the rest of his life. I thought he was out of his mind. I asked him about the dangers on the New York City streets, and he laughed. He reminded me that we were both raised in tough neighborhoods and that we instinctively knew how to handle ourselves and handle tough situations. I still thought he was crazy. He had stopped going to school and joined the police department. I had already finished college and was making good money in the career I had chosen.

Remember when I said that dreams and goals change? Well, this is the second example. I thought about my friend for weeks. I went to work day after day with retirement and the choices he had made on my mind. I began looking at the older guys in the office where I worked, how they struggled, were always tired, and were unhappy in their mundane jobs. I began to recall how much I loved playing cops and robbers as a kid, rolling on the floor, coming up shooting my toy gun, and taking cover from the imaginary bad guy. How nice it would be to retire in 20 years, start a new career, open a business, or just do whatever I wanted to do. How great it would be to be in a career that I not only liked but loved. The excitement, the fun, and the thrill of being a cop in New York City had me giving it some serious thought. All that and I would get a gun, a real police badge, and the ability to continue my education for free or rise through the ranks. Wow!

It was still a tough decision. I began to think of my mother, who had passed away months before I finished college; how she never got to see me graduate; how so many of the dreams and plans she had were never realized because she died young. It made me realize that life is short and that tomorrow is not guaranteed. To grasp life by the horns and try your best to get everything that you want in life. Accomplish every dream, every goal, kick down every door if you must, and never give up. I found my motivation to step outside of myself and the comfortable life I was beginning, to take chances. This motivation led me to join the police department, become an NYPD detective, get into the Homicide unit, rise through the detective ranks to earn First Grade status, and take advantage of those scholarships by getting my master's degree during the process.

    Sure, the police academy was tough, the job was tough, the hours were tough, and this put strains on my new-at-the-time marriage, but I was happy. I loved my job, my career, my life. Not liked – loved! I pushed through many obstacles and barriers to get to where I was. I was proud of myself, I was proud of what I had accomplished. However, anyone who knew me knew that would not be enough for me. My goal had become to retire, continue my education, teach others, and something of my own – a business. Near the end of my police career, while working as a Homicide detective in Manhattan, I decided to begin my exit strategy. I decided to go back to school to pursue my Ph.D. with the hopes of teaching at the college level. My plate was so full, I felt like it would make me sick, but I had to push on. I was motivated to succeed. I began teaching part time while working on my Ph.D. and struggling to get promoted in the Homicide squad.

    I recall all the cool shows and series that were on TV at the time that all the guys in the office would talk about the day after they aired. They would ask me if I saw the show and I would always respond, "I don't watch TV, I don't have time for TV." They would look at me like I was crazy. I'm not sure if they thought I was anti-social, or if they understood my struggle and the sacrifices I was making. The same thing happened when it came to going out after work for drinks and attending family events. I knew that I was making a sacrifice to accomplish the goal that I had set for myself. I knew that for my dreams to come true, I had to maintain my motivation and be willing to step outside of the norm and do things differently.

My motivation has paid off. I earned the promotion to Detective First Grade, retired with 23 years on the job, finished my Ph.D., am teaching undergraduate criminal justice courses, and have started my consulting business. All this is to say: No matter what the process, no matter what obstacles exist, be motivated to achieve your dreams and goals. Motivation will get you there. Forward Motion!

Chapter Nine

The Downside of Ambition

There can be a downside to this. When you find yourself being the only one in a group who thinks a certain way, the one who'd rather stay in than go out to the club or a bar, or the one who'd rather stop after one drink instead of getting shit-faced and unable to function the next day, you tend to find yourself alone after a while. This can create a lot of lonely times. Are you prepared for that?

There are ways to deal with and offset this possible outcome, but you will have to accept it first and then prepare. To be honest with you, most of the people who have the ambition and drive that is described in this book are already familiar with this kind of separation and loneliness. It has become a part of our lives. We are used to people not understanding us, being envious of us, being jealous of us, or those who are just plain sick and tired of hearing us talk about what we are going to do or going to be. For those of you who have just realized the power you possess through ambition and drive, get used to it and accept it because it goes with the territory.

What you are going to have to learn is who you are, who you are dealing with, and how to separate things. If you have been sharing your dreams with someone who just stares at you when you tell them what you want to do, or with someone who always asks you: "Why do you have to do that? Why do you want to do that?" – trust me, that is not the person you should be talking to. If they understood they wouldn't be asking you those types of questions. They would either be partnering with you to help build your dream or expressing a dream of their own. Trust me. I'll say it again: Trust me. You will eventually pull away from this person or be forced to separate from this person, one way or another. That separation may not mean that you push this person completely out of your life. You simply do not turn to this particular friend for inspiration, help, or understanding when things related to your dreams and goals go astray.

This kind of drive can be dangerous. It can make you feel as if you do not have time for someone who does not function and think as you do. Over time, you may begin to feel that this person can be a hindrance to your success. You may feel as though you cannot have a person like that in your life if you want to succeed. If this is someone whom you have deep feelings for, such as a partner, watch out! It can mess with your head and bring a lot of unnecessary confusion into your life. I urge you to fight the feeling of simply dismissing this person from your life altogether. I urge you to keep this person in your life and simply determine his or her positioning with regards to your life. Understand that not all people think as you do, have the dreams you have, or have reached the point in life to have made a commitment to go after their dreams.

Whether you are dealing with family, friends, or loved ones who do not see what you see, I urge you to simply limit their access and input into your world. Remember, you do not have to throw your family, friend, or partner to the wayside; what you *can* do is assess this person's usefulness in your life. What I mean by this is that everyone serves a purpose in your life. Your spouse or partner may be the source of love and affection. Your friend may be a great listener when you have relationship problems, or the person you go to when you want to let your hair down or laugh, or the person you go to for financial advice. Your family members may be the ones who get all the relatives together for birthdays, holidays, and family reunions. These people have a purpose. Ignoring them may not be the smartest or healthiest thing to do and may place a void in another part of your life. Just remember though, you do not have to share your dreams and ambition with them. They may not be *that* person. However, they still may have an important place in your life.

    Not everyone looks at things like this or needs to, but it can be helpful to do so when needed. Some can manage the friendships and relationships in their lives differently; some can juggle more than others. However, to those of you who realize that you have been serious about your dreams and goals, I ask you to look at your life and your relationships.

You may be surprised to find that this chapter pertains to you.

Forward Motion!

Chapter Ten

Never Give Up! NEVER!!!

No matter how hard it gets, never give up! If you end up broke, homeless, and destitute, don't give up! This is a very important premise. You must have the determination to reach your goals at any cost. Nothing should ever cause you to give up; nothing should cause you to feel as if you've failed.

Every mishap or unfortunate occurrence should be seen as merely an obstacle along the path to success. When you come upon an obstacle, you should push it aside, go under it, over it, around it, or even bust through it if you must. This is the place where you can take that step back, which was discussed in previous chapters, but you do not give up! It's an obstacle; that's all. The definition of an obstacle is something or someone blocking, hindering, opposing, or standing in the way of progress. Remember, it's just something that is going in the opposite direction you are going. It is simply something that is standing in your way. None of these things should make you stop. Pause, maybe, but never stop. And that pause is only to evaluate the situation.

If you feel strongly about your dream, your vision, nothing will stop you. In fact, if you've planned as you should, you should be expecting most of the obstacles that pop up. Your plan should include the "what ifs" that you should be prepared for. However, you must also be prepared for the unexpected obstacles, and there will be always be obstacles.

To put this into perspective, I will provide an example that should provide clarity. Many of us are immigrants to this country, whether it's first, second, third, or whatever generation. At some point in the past, our ancestors came to this country for a better life. What if they never tried? What if they did not have the determination to leave their country? What if they let fear or doubt stand in their way? Where would they be? Where would you be? Where would your family be? It is that determination, planning, vision, and forward thinking that changed the course of your family. That is what is needed for any plan or idea that you want to succeed at.

Now don't get me wrong: I do understand that some of us have ancestors who were brought to this country against their will. If that is the case in your family's history, you also have a lot to be grateful for. Your ancestors were determined to make it against tremendous odds, they envisioned a brighter future, and their forward thinking allowed them to push through the difficult times and sub-human conditions. Where would you be if your family had given up? Where would your family be if your ancestors had given up?

Regardless of your starting point, current or past financial situation, lack of mastery of the English language, or current or past educational situation – never question the fact that you have inside of you the ability to succeed. Never let race, religion, color, creed, or gender stand in the way of getting and being whatever you want to be. Remember: Plan, plan, and plan some more:

1. Figure out what it takes to get what you want in life – your dream, your goal.
2. Develop a plan to obtain whatever you need to accomplish that dream or goal.
3. Put the plan into action and make it happen.

The plan, after you've figured out what you want, may include going to school to get a specific education. Or, it may not be a formal education, it may include getting training in the area you plan to succeed in. Whatever it is, get it, find it, and make it happen – anything else is an excuse.

You must understand, your progress and success depends on it.

Forward Motion!

Final Thoughts… In Conclusion

The first thing to understand about this process is that if you are reading this book you either have an interest in becoming successful at something, have repeatedly tried to become successful, or are preparing for success in some way, shape, or form. By reading this book, you have taken a positive step in the journey towards your success. You have put fear aside or are learning to put fear aside and let ambition, determination, and perseverance lead you. Your success could be any endeavor you value and desire in your life. It could be completing college and earning a degree; it could be leaving your job and starting your own business; it could be purchasing real estate to rent, renovate, or own; or it could be any dream or goal that you desire.

One of the important aspects of this book to remember during your quest is that there will be people who try to insert negativity into your journey. Whether intentional or not, there will be those who question why you must be different, and there will be those who simply do not understand your drive and determination. Additionally, there will be haters – those who do not want to see you succeed. This negativity, and the haters, can come in the form of family, friends, or associates. This book provides several options for dealing with each one. Either way, turn this negativity into a positive. Use all of this as strength to push on, to push forward, and to continue the forward motion to your dreams.

Another important aspect is being careful not to let the actions of others and association with others bring you down. There are many individuals in jail or off track who are unable to continue their desired journey because of something someone else did or the association they had with the wrong people. You do not want your life to be turned upside down, put off track, or have surmountable obstacles added because you were in the wrong place at the wrong time. Think things through, consider all options and possibilities, and make educated decisions pertaining to your life. I often (not to be fearful of life) look at the worst-case scenario in a situation and determine my course of action based on the possible outcome. The least amount of preparation in this scenario should be a mental plan to abort ship should signs become apparent that things are heading in that dreaded direction.

The choices you make are paramount. Staying away from drugs, alcohol, and all the other vices that life offers is a good start. These vices can allow you to lose control of your life and throw your dreams away. Education is another choice that should be part of decisions made during this process. If your dreams require education, don't put it off. Do it now. Whether it's college, skill training, or some form of licensing course, get it done and be sure to take your situation all in and learn from it. Education is a marvelous thing. If nothing else, it provides you with the ability to think outside the box, to understand and see the possibilities of life and the world we live in. Education can be the tool that will help you understand that any goal is achievable.

So remember: Don't be afraid to go it alone, don't let anything get in your way. Big or small, stay motivated, and never give up! NEVER!

CONTINUE IN A FORWARD MOTION!!!

About the Author...

The author of this book, Dr. Alfred S. Titus, Jr., grew up in Jamaica, Queens, New York. Alfred attended Aviation High School in his early pursuit of becoming an Airline Pilot. After high school, he obtained his bachelor's degree in Electro-Mechanical Computer Technology in his new pursuit to be part of the technology revolution. After working in the computer field for a few years he decided to pursue his life-long dream of being a law enforcement agent. He joined the New York City Police Department with the intention of making a difference and touching lives. Police Officer Titus began by working in the subways in Harlem, New York, and Washington Heights, New York, where he learned the community and the job first hand. Police Officer Titus was an active and dedicated police officer who quickly moved into plainclothes assignments. His diligence provided him the opportunity to work with the Manhattan Robbery Squad where he earned the rank of Detective. Detective Titus later transferred to the Manhattan Night-Watch

Squad where his attention to detail on several high-profile cases gained the attention of the Manhattan South Homicide Squad. Within a year, Detective Titus became a member of the Manhattan South Homicide Squad, a prestigious unit in NYPD's Detective Bureau. During his 11 years in the Homicide Squad, Detective Titus led numerous high-profile cases, ending in arrest, and conviction. His success in Homicide earned him two promotions within the Detective rank, allowing him to reach the top accolades of Detective First Grade. While in Homicide, Detective Titus became a member of NYPD's elite Hostage Negotiation team and was trained as a Negotiator. As a Hostage Negotiator, he helped to save the lives of several emotionally disturbed persons and persons in crisis.

In addition to the successes in his career, while working in the NYPD, Detective Titus earned his master's degree through a Police Department scholarship. He also began work as a part-time Adjunct Lecturer at John Jay College of Criminal Justice while working towards his Ph.D. in Public Policy and Administration with a specialization in Criminal Justice, all while juggling the demanding schedule and workload of the Homicide Squad. Detective Titus retired from the NYPD in July 2016 to complete his doctorate and pursue a second career as an educator and consultant. He completed his doctoral dissertation in 2017 and earned the title of Dr. Alfred S. Titus, Jr., Ph.D.

Forward Motion… the Keys to Progress and Success! is the first book by Dr. Alfred S. Titus, Jr. He has created a consulting firm, A. Titus Consulting, LLC, to pursue goals which include creating additional literature addressing issues in law enforcement, research related to criminal justice, educating our youth, and all things related to social change and empowerment.

Dr. Titus' earlier articles and works are listed below:

Ph.D. Dissertation:
Realigning Community Policing in a Homeland Security Era
http://scholarworks.waldenu.edu/dissertations/4106/

Who is Looking Out for Us... the Lowering of Police Hiring Standards.

www.linkedin.com/pulse/who-looking-out-us-lowering-police-hiring-standards-alfred-titus-mpa

Transparency in Policing

http://jpublicpolicy.com/2016/03/05/tramsparancy-in-policy-through-nypds-citizens-police-academy/#more-1139

Dr. Alfred S. Titus, Jr. can be contacted for panel discussions, speaking engagements, and media consulting at:

A. Titus Consulting, LLC
P.O. Box 1056
Valley Stream, NY 11582
Email: ATitus@ATitusConsulting.com
Website: www.ATitusConsulting.com

Made in the USA
Middletown, DE
14 March 2018